THE
LITTLE BOOK OF
SELF-CARE
— FOR —
LEO

Simple Ways to Refresh and
Restore—According
to the Stars

CONSTANCE STELLAS

ADAMS MEDIA
NEW YORK   LONDON   TORONTO   SYDNEY   NEW DELHI

Adams Media
An Imprint of Simon & Schuster, Inc.
57 Littlefield Street
Avon, Massachusetts 02322

First Adams Media hardcover edition January 2019

ADAMS MEDIA and colophon are trademarks of Simon & Schuster.

For information about special discounts for bulk purchases, please contact Simon & Schuster Special Sales at 1-866-506-1949 or business@simonandschuster.com.

The Simon & Schuster Speakers Bureau can bring authors to your live event. For more information or to book an event contact the Simon & Schuster Speakers Bureau at 1-866-248-3049 or visit our website at www.simonspeakers.com.

Interior design by Sylvia McArdle
Interior images © Getty Images; Clipart.com

Manufactured in the United States of America

5 2020

Library of Congress Cataloging-in-Publication Data
Names: Stellas, Constance, author.
Title: The little book of self-care for Leo / Constance Stellas.
Description: Avon, Massachusetts: Adams Media, 2019.
Series: Astrology self-care.
Identifiers: LCCN 2018038277 | ISBN 9781507209721 (hc) | ISBN 9781507209738 (ebook)
Subjects: LCSH: Leo (Astrology) | Self-care, Health--Miscellanea.
Classification: LCC BF1727.35 .S74 2019 | DDC 133.5/266--dc23
LC record available at https://lccn.loc.gov/2018038277

ISBN 978-1-5072-0972-1
ISBN 978-1-5072-0973-8 (ebook)

Dedication

To my bold, fun, and longtime Leo friends,
Martha and Marina.

CONTENTS

Acknowledgments

I would like to thank Karen Cooper and everyone at Adams Media who helped with this book. To Brendan O'Neill, Katie Corcoran Lytle, Eileen Mullan, Meredith O'Hayre, Casey Ebert, Sylvia Davis, and everyone else who worked on the manuscripts. To Frank Rivera, Colleen Cunningham, and Katrina Machado for their work on the book's cover and interior design. I appreciated your team spirit and eagerness to dive into the riches of astrology.

Introduction

It's time for you to have a little *"me" time*—powered by the zodiac. By tapping into your Sun sign's astrological and elemental energies, *The Little Book of Self-Care for Leo* brings star-powered strength and cosmic relief to your life with self-care guidance tailored specifically for you.

While you may enjoy being the center of attention, Leo, this book focuses on your true self. This book provides information on how to incorporate self-care into your life while teaching you just how important astrology is to your overall self-care routine. You'll learn more about yourself as you learn about your sign and its governing element, fire. Then you can relax, rejuvenate, and stay balanced with more than one hundred self-care ideas and activities perfect for your Leo personality.

From meditating with crystals to attending a music festival, you will find plenty of ways to heal your mind, body, and active spirit. Now, let the stars be your self-care guide!

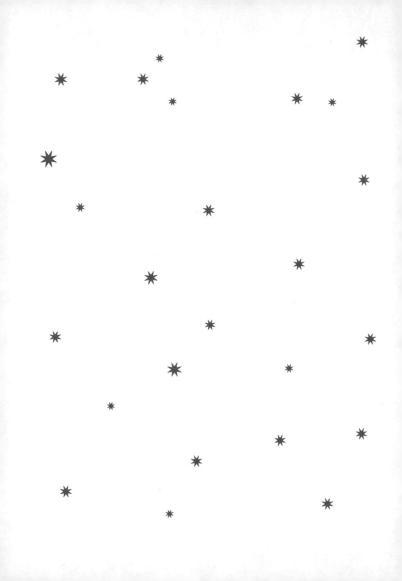

PART 1

SIGNS, ELEMENTS, AND SELF-CARE

CHAPTER 1

WHAT IS SELF-CARE?

*

Astrology gives insights into whom to love, when to charge forward into new beginnings, and how to succeed in whatever you put your mind to. When paired with self-care, astrology can also help you relax and reclaim that part of yourself that tends to get lost in the bustle of the day. In this chapter you'll learn what self-care is—for you. (No matter your sign, self-care is more than just lit candles and quiet reflection, though these activities may certainly help you find the renewal that you seek.) You'll also learn how making a priority of personalized self-care activities can benefit you in ways you may not even have thought of. Whether you're a Leo, a Pisces, or a Taurus, you deserve rejuvenation and renewal that's customized to your sign—this chapter reveals where to begin.

What Self-Care Is

Self-care is any activity that you do to take care of yourself. It rejuvenates your body, refreshes your mind, or realigns your spirit. It relaxes and refuels you. It gets you ready for a new day or a fresh start. It's the practices, rituals, and meaningful activities that you do, just for you, that help you feel safe, grounded, happy, and fulfilled.

The activities that qualify as self-care are amazingly unique and personalized to who you are, what you like, and, in large part, what your astrological sign is. If you're asking questions about what self-care practices are best for those ruled by fire and born under the bold eye of Leo, you'll find answers—and restoration—in Part 2. But, no matter which of those self-care activities speak to you and your unique place in the universe on any given day, it will fall into one of the following self-care categories—each of which pertains to a different aspect of your life:

* Physical self-care
* Emotional self-care
* Social self-care
* Mental self-care
* Spiritual self-care
* Practical self-care

When you practice all of these unique types of self-care—and prioritize your practice to ensure you are choosing the best options for your unique sign and governing element—know that you are actively working to create the version of yourself that the universe intends you to be.

Physical Self-Care

When you practice physical self-care, you make the decision to look after and restore the one physical body that has been bestowed upon you. Care for it. Use it in the best way you can imagine, for that is what the universe wishes you to do. You can't light the world on fire or move mountains if you're not doing everything you can to take care of your physical health.

Emotional Self-Care

Emotional self-care is when you take the time to acknowledge and care for your inner self, your emotional well-being. Whether you're angry or frustrated, happy or joyful, or somewhere in between, emotional self-care happens when you choose to sit with your emotions: when you step away from the noise of daily life that often drowns out or tamps down your authentic self. Emotional self-care lets you see your inner you as the cosmos intend. Once you identify your true emotions, you can either accept them and continue to move forward on your journey or you can try to change any negative emotions for the better. The more you acknowledge your feelings and practice emotional self-care, the more you'll feel the positivity that the universe and your life holds for you.

Social Self-Care

You practice social self-care when you nurture your relationships with others, be they friends, coworkers, or family members. In today's hectic world it's easy to let relationships fall to the wayside, but it's so important to share your life with others—and let others share their lives with you. Social self-care is reciprocal and often karmic. The support and love that you put out into the universe through social self-care is given back to you by those you socialize with—often tenfold.

Mental Self-Care

Mental self-care is anything that keeps your mind working quickly and critically. It helps you cut through the fog of the day, week, or year and ensures that your quick wit and sharp mind are intact and working the way the cosmos intended. Making sure your mind is fit helps you problem-solve, decreases stress since you're not feeling overwhelmed, and keeps you feeling on top of your mental game—no matter your sign or your situation.

Spiritual Self-Care

Spiritual self-care is self-care that allows you to tap into your soul and the soul of the universe and uncover its secrets. Rather than focusing on a particular religion or set of religious beliefs, these types of self-care activities reconnect you with a higher power: the sense that something out there is bigger than you. When you meditate, you connect. When you pray, you connect. Whenever you do something that allows you to experience and marry yourself to the vastness that is the cosmos, you practice spiritual self-care.

Practical Self-Care

Self-care is what you do to take care of yourself, and practical self-care, while not as expansive as the other types, is made up of the seemingly small day-to-day tasks that bring you peace and accomplishment. These practical self-care rituals are important, but are often overlooked. Scheduling a doctor's appointment that you've been putting off is practical self-care. Getting your hair cut is practical self-care. Anything you can check off your list of things to be accomplished gives you a sacred space to breathe and allows the universe more room to bring a beautiful sense of cosmic fulfillment your way.

What Self-Care Isn't

Self-care is restorative. Self-care is clarifying. Self-care is whatever you need to do to make yourself feel secure in the universe.

Now that you know what self-care is, it's also important that you're able to see what self-care isn't. Self-care is not something that you force yourself to do because you think it will be good for you. Some signs are energy in motion and sitting still goes against their place in the universe. Those signs won't feel refreshed by lying in a hammock or sitting down to meditate. Other signs aren't able to ground themselves unless they've found a self-care practice that protects their cosmic need for peace and quiet. Those signs won't find parties, concerts, and loud venues soothing or satisfying. If a certain ritual doesn't bring you peace, clarity, or satisfaction, then it's not right for your sign and you should find something that speaks to you more clearly.

There's a difference though between not finding satisfaction in a ritual that you've tried and not wanting to try a self-care activity because you're tired or stuck in a comfort zone. Sometimes going to the gym or meeting up with friends is the self-care practice that you need to experience—whether engaging in it feels like a downer or not. So consider how you feel when you're actually doing the activity. If it feels invigorating to get on the treadmill or you feel delight when you actually catch up with your friend, the ritual is doing what it should be doing and clearing space for you—among other benefits...

The Benefits of Self-Care

The benefits of self-care are boundless and there's none that's superior to helping you put rituals in place to feel more at home in your body, in your spirit, and in your unique home in the cosmos. There are, however, other benefits to engaging in the practice of self-care that you should know.

Rejuvenates Your Immune System

No matter which rituals are designated for you by the stars, your sign, and its governing element, self-care helps both your body and mind rest, relax, and recuperate. The practice of self-care activates the parasympathetic nervous system (often called the rest and digest system), which slows your heart rate, calms the body, and overall helps your body relax and release tension. This act of decompression gives your body the space it needs to build up and strengthen your immune system, which protects you from illness.

Helps You Reconnect—with Yourself

When you practice the ritual of self-care—especially when you customize this practice based on your personal sign and governing element—you learn what you like to do and what you need to do to replenish yourself. Knowing yourself better, and allowing yourself the time and space that you need to focus on your personal needs and desires, gives you the gifts of self-confidence and self-knowledge. Setting time aside to focus on your needs also helps you put busy, must-do things aside, which gives you time to reconnect with yourself and who you are deep inside.

Increases Compassion

Perhaps one of the most important benefits of creating a self-care ritual is that, by focusing on yourself, you become more compassionate to others as well. When you truly take the time to care for yourself and make yourself and your importance in the universe a priority in your own life, you're then able to care for others and see their needs and desires in a new way. You can't pour from an empty dipper, and self-care allows you the space and clarity to do what you can to send compassion out into the world.

Starting a Self-Care Routine

Self-care should be treated as a ritual in your life, something you make the time to pause for, no matter what. You are important. You deserve rejuvenation and a sense of relaxation. You need to open your soul to the gifts that the universe is giving you, and self-care provides you with a way to ensure you're ready to receive those gifts. To begin a self-care routine, start by making yourself the priority. Do the customized rituals in Part 2 with intention, knowing the universe has already given them to you, by virtue of your sign and your governing element.

Now that you understand the role that self-care will hold in your life, let's take a closer look at the connection between self-care and astrology.

CHAPTER 2

SELF-CARE AND ASTROLOGY

✳

Astrology is the study of the connection between the objects in the heavens (the planets, the stars) and what happens here on earth. Just as the movements of the planets and other heavenly bodies influence the ebb and flow of the tides, so do they influence you—your body, your mind, your spirit. This relationship is ever present and is never more important—or personal—than when viewed through the lens of self-care.

In this chapter you'll learn how the locations of these celestial bodies at the time of your birth affect you and define the self-care activities that will speak directly to you as a Leo, an Aries, a Capricorn, or any of the other zodiac signs. You'll see how the zodiac influences every part of your being and why ignoring its lessons can leave you feeling frustrated and unfulfilled. You'll also realize that, when you perform the rituals of self-care based on your sign, the wisdom of the cosmos will lead you down a path of fulfillment and restoration—to the return of who *you* really are, deep inside.

Zodiac Polarities

In astrology, all signs are mirrored by other signs that are on the opposite side of the zodiac. This polarity ensures that the zodiac is balanced and continues to flow with an unbreakable, even stream of energy. There are two different polarities in the zodiac and each is called by a number of different names:

* Yang/masculine/positive polarity
* Yin/feminine/negative polarity

Each polar opposite embodies a number of opposing traits, qualities, and attributes that will influence which self-care practices will work for or against your sign and your own personal sense of cosmic balance.

Yang
Whether male or female, those who fall under yang, or masculine, signs are extroverted and radiate their energy outward. They are spontaneous, active, bold, and fearless. They move forward in life with the desire to enjoy everything the

world has to offer to them, and they work hard to transfer their inspiration and positivity to others so that those individuals may experience the same gifts that the universe offers them. All signs governed by the fire and air elements are yang and hold the potential for these dominant qualities. We will refer to them with masculine pronouns. These signs are:

* Aries
* Leo
* Sagittarius

* Gemini
* Libra
* Aquarius

There are people who hold yang energy who are introverted and retiring. However, by practicing self-care that is customized for your sign and understanding the potential ways to use your energy, you can find a way—perhaps one that's unique to you—to claim your native buoyancy and dominance and engage with the path that the universe opens for you.

Yin

Whether male or female, those who fall under yin, or feminine, signs are introverted and radiate inwardly. They draw people and experiences to them rather than seeking people and experiences in an extroverted way. They move forward in life with an energy that is reflective, receptive, and focused on communication and achieving shared goals. All signs governed by the earth and water elements are yin and hold the potential for these reflective qualities. We will refer to them with feminine pronouns. These signs are:

* Taurus
* Virgo
* Capricorn

* Cancer
* Scorpio
* Pisces

As there are people with yang energy who are introverted and retiring, there are also people with yin energy who are outgoing and extroverted. And by practicing self-care rituals that speak to your particular sign, energy, and governing body, you will reveal your true self and the balance of energy will be maintained.

Governing Elements

Each astrological sign has a governing element that defines their energy orientation and influences both the way the sign moves through the universe and relates to self-care. The elements are fire, earth, air, and water. All the signs in each element share certain characteristics, along with having their own sign-specific qualities:

* **Fire:** Fire signs are adventurous, bold, and energetic. They enjoy the heat and warm environments and look to the sun and fire as a means to recharge their depleted batteries. They're competitive, outgoing, and passionate. The fire signs are Aries, Leo, and Sagittarius.
* **Earth:** Earth signs all share a common love and tendency toward a practical, material, sensual, and economic orientation. The earth signs are Taurus, Virgo, and Capricorn.
* **Air:** Air is the most ephemeral element and those born under this element are thinkers, innovators, and communicators. The air signs are Gemini, Libra, and Aquarius.
* **Water:** Water signs are instinctual, compassionate, sensitive, and emotional. The water signs are Cancer, Scorpio, and Pisces.

Chapter 3 teaches you all about the ways your specific governing element influences and drives your connection to your cosmically harmonious self-care rituals, but it's important that you realize how important these elemental traits are to your self-care practice and to the activities that will help restore and reveal your true self.

Sign Qualities

Each of the astrological elements governs three signs. Each of these three signs is also given its own quality or mode, which corresponds to a different part of each season: the beginning, the middle, or the end.

* **Cardinal signs:** The cardinal signs initiate and lead in each season. Like something that is just starting out, they are actionable, enterprising, and assertive, and are born leaders. The cardinal signs are Aries, Cancer, Libra, and Capricorn.
* **Fixed signs:** The fixed signs come into play when the season is well established. They are definite, consistent, reliable, motivated by principles, and powerfully stubborn. The fixed signs are Taurus, Leo, Scorpio, and Aquarius.
* **Mutable signs:** The mutable signs come to the forefront when the seasons are changing. They are part of one season, but also part of the next. They are adaptable, versatile, and flexible. The mutable signs are Gemini, Virgo, Sagittarius, and Pisces.

Each of these qualities tells you a lot about yourself and who you are. They also give you invaluable information about the types of self-care rituals that your sign will find the most intuitive and helpful.

Ruling Planets

In addition to qualities and elements, each specific sign is ruled by a particular planet that lends its personality to those born under that sign. Again, these sign-specific traits give you valuable insight into the personality of the signs and the self-care rituals that may best rejuvenate them. The signs that correspond to each planet—and the ways that those planetary influences determine your self-care options—are as follows:

* **Aries:** Ruled by Mars, Aries is passionate, energetic, and determined.
* **Taurus:** Ruled by Venus, Taurus is sensual, romantic, and fertile.
* **Gemini:** Ruled by Mercury, Gemini is intellectual, changeable, and talkative.
* **Cancer:** Ruled by the Moon, Cancer is nostalgic, emotional, and home loving.
* **Leo:** Ruled by the Sun, Leo is fiery, dramatic, and confident.
* **Virgo:** Ruled by Mercury, Virgo is intellectual, analytical, and responsive.
* **Libra:** Ruled by Venus, Libra is beautiful, romantic, and graceful.
* **Scorpio:** Ruled by Mars and Pluto, Scorpio is intense, powerful, and magnetic.
* **Sagittarius:** Ruled by Jupiter, Sagittarius is optimistic, boundless, and larger than life.

* **Capricorn:** Ruled by Saturn, Capricorn is wise, patient, and disciplined.
* **Aquarius:** Ruled by Uranus, Aquarius is independent, unique, and eccentric.
* **Pisces:** Ruled by Neptune and Jupiter, Pisces is dreamy, sympathetic, and idealistic.

A Word on Sun Signs

When someone is a Leo, Aries, Sagittarius, or any of the other zodiac signs, it means that the sun was positioned in this constellation in the heavens when they were born. Your Sun sign is a dominant factor in defining your personality, your best self-care practices, and your soul nature. Every person also has the position of the Moon, Mercury, Venus, Mars, Jupiter, Saturn, Uranus, Neptune, and Pluto. These planets can be in any of the elements: fire signs, earth signs, air signs, or water signs. If you have your entire chart calculated by an astrologer or on an Internet site, you can see the whole picture and learn about all your elements. Someone born under Leo with many signs in another element will not be as concentrated in the fire element as someone with five or six planets in Leo. Someone born in Pisces with many signs in another element will not be as concentrated in the water element as someone with five or six planets in Pisces. And so on. Astrology is a complex system and has many shades of meaning. For our purposes looking at the self-care practices designated by your Sun sign, or what most people consider *their* sign, will give you the information you need to move forward and find fulfillment and restoration.

ESSENTIAL ELEMENTS: FIRE

✳

F ire gives us heat, warmth, and light. And those who have fire as their governing element—like you, Leo, as well as Aries and Sagittarius—all have a special energy signature and connection with fire that guides all aspects of their lives. Fire signs are drawn to the flames in all its varied forms and environments whether this gift comes from the sun, an outdoor campfire, or a cozy fireplace fire, and their approach to self-care reflects their relationship with this fiery element. Let's take a look at the mythological importance of the sun, as well as the basic characteristics of the three fire signs, and what they all have in common when it comes to self-care.

The Mythology of Fire

In astrology, fire is considered the first element of creation. Perhaps it was primitive man's way of understanding the big bang, or maybe fire just made a clear-cut difference between living in the wild and gathering together in human communities. In Greek mythology the immortal Prometheus angered the gods by stealing fire for the mortals he had such affection for down on earth. As punishment he was chained to a rock and Zeus sent an eagle to eat his liver. Magically, this liver regenerated every day and the eagle kept devouring it. Prometheus was later released from this curse, but the gift of fire that he gave to mankind was not completely free of conflict.

Fire was—and remains—an essential part of civilized life, but it also gives humans the ability to forge weapons of war. Fire warms a home, cooks a meal, and restores and enlivens the spirit, but too much fire can destroy. All fire signs feel this duality between the creative and destructive force of their fire power energy, and this duality drives their likes and dislikes, personality traits, and approaches to self-care.

The Element of Fire

The fire signs are known as the inspirational signs because their enthusiasm and buoyant personalities help them to cheer themselves and others on to great success. They also represent the spiritual side of human nature and their sense of intuition is strong; fire signs often have hunches about themselves and others, and if they follow these hunches, they typically achieve whatever they set out to do. For example, Aries inspires the spark that pioneers a project or endeavor. Leo is a leader who inspires his circle of friends, family, or colleagues to keep their eyes on the goal at hand, even when things get tough. And Sagittarius is an idealist and searches (and helps others search) for truth.

Astrological Symbols

The astrological symbols (also called the zodiacal symbols) of the fire signs also give you hints as to how the fire signs move through the world. All of the fire signs are represented by animals of power and determination, which ties right back to their shared fiery element:

* Aries is the Ram
* Leo is the Lion
* Sagittarius is the Centaur (half horse/half man)

Each fire sign's personality and subsequent approaches to self-care connect to the qualities of these representative animals. For example, the Ram is determined and confident. The Lion is king of the jungle and boldly defends his turf. And the Centaur, also called the Archer, shoots his arrows of truth and moves powerfully against any attempts to rein him in.

Signs and Seasonal Modes

Each of the elements in astrology has a sign that corresponds to a different part of each season.

* **Cardinal:** Aries, as the first fire sign, is the harbinger of spring, and the spring equinox begins the astrological year. Aries is called a cardinal fire sign because it leads the season.

* **Fixed:** Leo, the second fire sign, occurs in midsummer when summer is well established. Leo is a fixed fire sign. The fixed signs are definite, motivated by principles, and powerfully stubborn.
* **Mutable:** Sagittarius is the sign that brings us from one season to the next. Sagittarius moves us from autumn to winter. These signs are called mutable. In terms of character the mutable signs are changeable and flexible.

If you know your element and whether you are a cardinal, fixed, or mutable sign, you know a lot about yourself. This is invaluable for self-care and is reflected in the customized fire sign self-care rituals found in Part 2.

Fire Signs and Self-Care

Self-care is incredibly important for fire signs. But learning how to set aside time for self-care takes discipline because fire doesn't want to stop. Fire elements have an incredible spark that lights up their minds, bodies, and spirits, but, as with fire, those born under this element frequently burn out. When this happens, making frequent pit stops to refuel, rest, and engage in self-care activities that are personalized for their element—like the ones found in Part 2—are what fire signs require to be stoked back to life.

Fire signs need to keep in mind that their self-care activities should be fun and varied; they don't want to get bored doing the same thing over and over again when there are so many different self-care options to try! The fire element crackles with enthusiasm and good spirits, and the more activity, socializing, and fun they can have, the better they like it and the easier it is for people born under this element to get fired up. Fire signs will easily follow any practice or activity that enhances playfulness. Variety in exercise, diet, décor, fashion, friendship, vacations, and socializing gives all fire elements the motivation to enjoy life, and without a good time life is a misery for these bold personalities.

The best way to approach self-care for fire signs is to make it a game. The fire signs have willpower to follow through on a plan if they decide something is worthwhile and they can enjoy it. The rules of the "game" don't matter as much as the sense of achieving a good score, beating the competition, or enjoying the process. For example, if a fire sign decides to do 10,000 steps in a day and finds at 5 p.m. that he is 1,000 steps short, his motivation to reach his goal would help him find a fun way to complete the program. Perhaps he will decide to march to music, skip, or hop his way to 10,000. A fire sign will get what he needs in two different ways through this type of self-care: he both wins the game and has fun doing it!

Maintaining that flame and steady inspiration is the goal of any self-care program. Play the game of taking care of your body, mind, and spirit, and not only will you benefit from your efforts, but you will also inspire others to follow you.

So now that you know what fire signs need to practice self-care, let's look at each of the fiery characteristics of Leo and how he can maintain his flame.

CHAPTER 4

SELF-CARE FOR LEO

✳

Dates: July 23–August 22
Element: Fire
Polarity: Yang
Quality: Fixed
Symbol: Lion
Ruler: The Sun

Leo is the second fire sign and the most vital sign in the zodiac. He reigns in summer when the sun is at its height. He is yang and a fixed sign, and his preferred self-care rituals line up with the traits associated with these cosmic designations. Leo's fire power is coiled and ready for action, and he has tremendous amounts of focused energy. These traits are also associated with the Lion, the unrivaled king of the jungle and Leo's impressive symbol. Like a lion, at his best Leo is the generous king sharing his warmth and magnanimity with all who come across his path. At his worst he is an attention seeker who has difficulty sharing the spotlight.

The Greek myth of Phaeton is one to consider for Leo. Phaeton, who was mortal on his mother's side, came to the Palace of the Sun to find out if the Sun God (the Sun is Leo's ruling planet) was indeed his father. The Sun God was touched by the boy's sincerity and told him that yes, he was his father. To prove his love, he offered the boy anything he wanted and Phaeton asked to drive his father's chariot of the Sun. The Sun God recognized that he had to fulfill his promise, but realizing that doing so would probably destroy the boy, he tried to dissuade him. Phaeton would not listen. He began his journey, but lost control of the reins, causing the chariot of the Sun to dip so near the earth that it threatened to burn everything in sight. The god Zeus intervened by throwing a thunderbolt at the chariot, striking Phaeton dead. The story's parallel with Leo's cosmic astrological personality traits is clear. If Leo lets his immature ego take the reins, there can be pain and meltdown. But if he is able to practice self-control, Leo can cooperate and share his enthusiasm and fiery, fun personality with others. The course of any Leo's life will be determined by the extent to which he can shine with other people.

Self-Care and Leo

Leo is a fire sign who is ruled by the Sun; therefore, he's active and adventurous and can be recharged by the sun, so look for lots of warm weather, outdoor self-care rituals. This sign is dramatic, confident, showy, and outgoing. Remember that Leo is symbolized by the Lion, so like a lion he is fierce and prideful, and loves taking care of his glorious mane. Hair care is seemingly a small part of life, but not for Leo. Leo's mane is his pride and joy. It is usually thick and wavy. He loves hair products, and any evidence that his hair is lackluster or falling out can propel him into examining how to take care of himself better. As the king of the jungle, Leo is also often enamored with royalty. All of these things combine to make engaging in self-care enjoyable, necessary, and desirable for this fire sign.

That said, Leo is the sign of the father—the leader of the pride—and, in traditional societies, the father as head of the household prayed for guidance to lead his family well. Both Leo men and women feel this responsibility for their family, friends, and circle of acquaintances and use their ability to inspire others to take care of their own. This pride in responsibility can weigh on those born under this sign, and it can make it difficult for Leo to really take the time to engage in a self-care routine, even though his excellent sense of intuition may tell him that he needs to. However, Leo loves to look good and enjoys indulging himself—no one is going to tell a Leo that he doesn't deserve something—so while getting Leo to practice self-care can be difficult, once he's started, it's tough to get Leo to stop.

Leo Rules the Heart and Spine

Leo rules over the spine and heart; self-care related to the spine, back, and heart is especially important. For Leo the bones of the spine aren't as important as the spinal cord, the pathway of energy in the body from bottom to top. This pathway in the Hindu tradition is called kundalini, or "vital energy," which travels from the base of the spine to the top of the head.

Leo has a natural intuition of what is good for him when all his energy is flowing up and down this light-filled pathway in the body, and (if he's paying attention) can use this intuition to choose self-care rituals that speak clearly to his sign and fire element. The best self-care practices for maintaining free energy flow for Leo are gentle stretches and yoga. Certain martial arts like Tai Chi are also beneficial. They are both graceful and powerful. Leo doesn't need an aggressive sport; he needs an elegant one such as aikido, fencing, or tennis. Leo lights up with any sport or exercise where he can shine individually and make use of his steady energy. Additionally, if Leo has aches and pains in any part of the back, it means there is a tension buildup that should be released. Self-care such as gentle chiropractic adjustments or cranial sacrum massage can easily help Leo keep in balance.

Leo also rules the heart. Phrases such as *brave heart, courageous heart,* or *he has a good heart* are frequently used to describe the Lion. He is king not only because of his power but also because of his care and warmth toward others. Eating a heart-healthy diet is an important self-care practice for Leo, and, in later years, those born under this sign should make time for annual checkups *and* stress tests to make sure the heart muscle is strong and steady.

That said, perhaps the more important part of heart care for Leo is emotional. Leo's heart expands with love the more he shares his fire power. His sign is synonymous with heart fire. He can give himself wholeheartedly to projects, to romance, and to his children—and this is the true meaning of Leo's gift to himself and others. Doing whatever you need to do to keep this most important soul quality front and center is the most vital type of self-care Leo can practice.

Leo and Self-Care Success

One pitfall for Leo's self-care program is that Leo does not enjoy programs that are rigid and mass produced. If he decides to meditate, for example, he will want to find the best teacher or group possible. And if the teacher is a little famous, it wouldn't hurt. Likewise, if there is prestige included in this group, it will please Leo's sense of entitlement and self-worth.

Another pitfall for a self-care program is lack of rewards. Leo needs to see progress as quickly as possible. The progress does not have to be measurable like so many pounds lost or reps performed, but Leo does like to see that something he wants to do or have is getting closer. For example, those pants that were too tight and now fit well and look great will encourage Leo to keep to an eating or fitness plan. If he feels discouraged, he can summon his willpower and try another approach. Leo can be very disciplined when pursuing a goal.

The best way for Leo to seek advice and to learn about self-care is to find a common bond with a knowledgeable equal who will help Leo shine more brilliantly. Leo can recognize his faults but does not take well to criticism. Leo does not like to be in a subservient or underling position to a doctor or professional. He is happy to learn and benefit from wisdom and guidance, especially if he is in the middle of stress or difficulties, but not at the expense of his own confidence and pride. Any whiff of competition and the Lion will stalk out of the room very quickly. Praise is the best approach. Leo doesn't need flattery, but a sincere recognition of Leo's very good qualities will help keep the Lion engaged and interested in any of his self-care rituals.

In terms of soul development, Leo is the sign of awareness of self. He always realizes and understands exactly how he's feeling, and his charisma and sense of self-confidence are palpable. Inside, however, those born under this fire sign can feel insecure, seek constant attention, and search for approval. This part of Leo's personality is sometimes hidden, though, as his pride keeps him from showing insecurity to those around him. The ability to balance these two parts of his personality throughout his life traces the soul growth of the Lion.

To keep developing his native soul qualities of generosity and leadership in his self-care program, Leo must feel that his efforts are appreciated. Leo needs a support group or a cheering section to boost and applaud his progress in developing body, mind, and spirit. This could literally be a gang of exercise buddies, a circle of meditation friends, or an intellectual group such as a book group. The essential part of self-care for Leo is that it involves other people who notice him, and any group like this has social possibilities, such as going to the juice bar or out to eat after exercising. This reinforces Leo's warmth and sparkle. He is not a loner.

Self-praise is another restorative way for Leo to encourage good self-care. He could give himself a round of applause for every healthful choice of food, for every good exercise session, for every generous action toward others. Self-care for Leo can be a natural outgrowth of the sign's pride in his appearance and making a good impression. Imagine that every day is opening night for the Leo show and your self-care program is the main attraction. This will motivate you to find self-care actions that are effective, fun, and workable. If all of this self-care prompts compliments and good attention, Leo will purr contentedly and maintain the habits of self-care forever.

Perhaps the most important pathway for self-care success, however, is when Leo can be the teacher. Leo is a natural-born teacher. You want to share your wisdom and knowledge with others—and as you teach others, you also inspire yourself to make self-care a priority in your life. So let's take a look at some self-care activities that are tailored specifically for you, Leo.

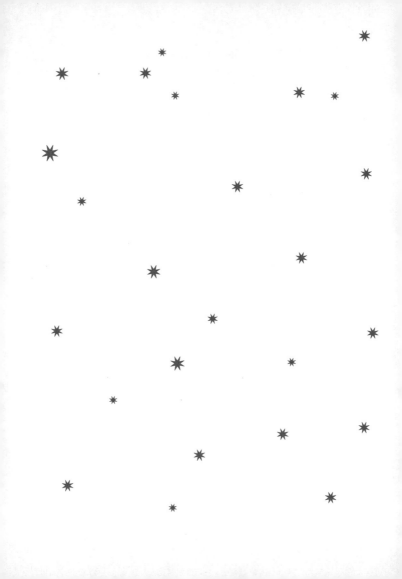

PART 2

SELF-CARE
RITUALS
— FOR —
LEO

37

Enjoy a Tequila Sunrise

Need to unwind, Leo? Sit back with a tequila sunrise. The tequila kick appeals to the adventurous side of Leo, and orange juice represents elements of the Sun, Leo's ruling planet.

To enjoy, combine 1½ ounces of tequila and ¾ cup of freshly squeezed orange juice in a jigger. Pour mixture over a glass of ice, and slowly add ½ ounce of grenadine syrup. Allow the grenadine to settle, giving your finished cocktail a dramatic aesthetic that appeals to Leo's showy nature. Enjoy this drink fit for a king!

Try Deep-Tissue Massage for Ultimate Relief

D o your sore muscles need a little TLC? Soothing touch is a great way to alleviate stress in your body and your mind. As a fire sign, ignite a different type of heat inside you by turning to the therapeutic benefits of deep-tissue massage. The warmth created by kneading muscle tissue and improved blood circulation can ease chronic tension, pain, and stiffness. And this deeply therapeutic ritual can help calm anxiety and worry as well.

Place your trust in an experienced massage therapist. Before your massage starts, tell them exactly how your body feels and what it needs to get better. Keep in mind that a deep-tissue massage should never be painful, so don't be afraid to speak up at any point during your massage. Communication is key.

Salute the Sun

Leo's confidence comes from his core, and yoga is an ideal way to manifest and strengthen Leo's most positive qualities. The best yoga posture for Leo as a fire sign? Naturally, a Sun Salutation. Greet the day with this practice.

There are many variations of this sequence, and you can modify the poses to suit your energy level on any given day. The more quickly you move through the sequence, the more stimulating it is. If you move through the poses more slowly, they can have a more calming effect. Look online or on your favorite yoga app for the Sun Salutation sequence to best suit your ability level and desire.

Decorate with
Peacock Feathers

Your home should be a reflection of yourself. Why not make it a regal retreat by working peacock feathers into your décor?

The peacock is a royal, beautiful bird that has become synonymous with the spotlight. Its aesthetic speaks to Leo's regal nature, so consider arranging a collection of peacock feathers in your entryway. When you come home at the end of a challenging day and you feel your crown slipping, you'll be greeted by a colorful display that will remind you of your innate Leo power.

Sweat Your Way to Relaxation

While we often think of heat as linked to passion and intensity, it can also be incredibly restorative and relaxing for fire signs. Embrace the calming effect of heat by seeking out a sauna at your local gym or spa. Take time to lounge in the warmth, allowing the sweat to cleanse your body of impurities. Breathe in the heat and feel the heat soften your muscles and increase your circulation. As the warmth envelopes your body, any pain and stress will melt away.

Can't find a sauna nearby? No problem. Turn on your shower to hot and let the water run for a few minutes. Be sure to close your windows and bathroom doors. Then get a comfy seat and kick back in your own at-home sauna for some rest and recuperation.

Meditate with Jacinth

This crystal, also known as zircon, occurs in a sunburst range of colors—orange-yellow, orange-red, or yellow-brown. The colors resonate well with Leo's fiery nature, but the affinity doesn't end there.

One way that naturally energetic Leo can benefit from jacinth is through the crystal's unique ability to prevent nightmares and ensure a deep and tranquil sleep.

Prepare yourself for rest. Wearing loose, comfortable nighttime clothing, sit or lie in a dimly lit room and hold the crystal in your left hand. Complete a series of ten cleansing breaths, focusing on releasing any pent-up energy through your exhalations. Keep your jacinth on your bedside table for restorative, restful sleep.

Burn Up the Competition

Fire signs thrive off of a little friendly competition—the key word being *friendly*! Engage your fiery competitive side in a healthy way by joining a community sports league of your choosing. You may find that team sports, like soccer, kickball, basketball, volleyball, or even a running group, suit you best. The sense of comradery can jump-start that passion inside you for action. Use the energy and excitement coming from your teammates as fuel. Just remember, it's only a game. No matter if your team wins or loses, the primary goal is to have fun and get your body moving.

Teach That Learning Is Power

It's as simple as ABC... As a fire sign, your ambition and passion for adventure has given you a lot of life experiences. Bring that passion and spirit you have for life to others by volunteering as a teacher in one capacity or another. This may mean becoming a mentor at a local after-school program, reading to children at the library, or teaching adults a special skill like painting or accounting at a community center. The choice is yours. But however you choose to go about it, know that instilling knowledge in others is an act of love and patience. A good teacher can inspire and motivate their students. And the benefit isn't just theirs. As a fire sign, engaging with a group can be incredibly fulfilling for you too. Take a survey of your many talents and see where you can help.

Soak Up the Sun

It's time to turn up the heat! Fire signs need vacations just like everyone else, but when planning yours, stick to warm, sunny destinations. You need the heat to feed your soul. Ditch your coat and look for vacation spots on the beach or in the desert, where the sun is strong and the temperatures soar. Fire signs are nourished by the heat, so soak up the rays for ultimate replenishment.

Keep your body and mind challenged with tons of adventures and new experiences. While taking some time to lounge and relax is totally fine, you need something to get your fire burning. Try to schedule at least one activity each day you are on vacation, whether that means going for a hike through canyons or learning to surf. The more out of your comfort zone you are, the more alive you'll feel.

Meditate On the Color Green

While Leo is very passionate, the heart is his most vulnerable area. You can protect your heart and strengthen your emotions through meditation, an important aspect of self-care no matter what your sign. Green is the heart chakra color, and it plays an important part in your meditation.

In a dimly lit room try to clear your mind as you focus on your breath. Each time you inhale, think of taking in the color green and directing its energy to your heart space.

Repeat this practice any time you feel particularly vulnerable, or need to balance your innate boldness with compassion and love.

Lead with Generosity

L eo leads with his heart, and this translates to a very generous nature. But in times of stress it is easy to abandon our natural gifts in favor of fight or flight. Shift your focus by making "I lead with generosity" your personal mantra, and repeat it often.

During difficult or stressful times (or any time you need to re-center), close your eyes and repeat "I lead with generosity" until you can feel your energy change. If you're in a setting where speaking aloud isn't possible, repeat the phrase in your head. You'll find that by reminding yourself of your innate gift, it will be easier to share with the world.

Embrace the Drama

———————

Leo has a flair for the dramatic—put it to good use! While chores like cleaning the house or making dinner may not *feel* like self-care, they are essential to your health and well-being. Turn mundane chores into an event by adding a soundtrack.

Instead of just turning on the radio, seek out music with a dramatic feel to get you in the mood. Show tunes are perfect! Turn the music up loud, and allow the strong voices and soaring strains to turn the ordinary into extraordinary. Your chores will go more quickly, and the emotion the music evokes will stay with you throughout your day.

Make 'Em Laugh

There's nothing quite like the power of a good belly laugh. Fire signs are extroverts by nature and love to entertain people with stories, songs, and even jokes. While you may not have an entire stand-up comedy set ready to go yet, all it takes is one simple joke to get someone laughing and improve their day. And that rush of joy coursing through your veins as your audience laughs is enough to raise any fire sign's temperature. Don't know any good jokes off the top of your head? Go for the classics or search online for some new material. And remember, it's all in the delivery!

Channel a Fellow Leo

Feeling down? Doubting yourself? Channel the energy of a fellow Leo to turn your mood around. Perhaps a dear Leo friend or family member has a swagger you've always admired—ask yourself what they would do in your shoes. By trying to adopt the headspace of someone else, you may see things through a different perspective.

If that doesn't work, look to the stars...as in celebrities! Barack Obama, Tom Brady, Madonna, and Mick Jagger are all Leos. Read some of their inspirational quotes. Watch an inspiring game or concert footage. Put on some of their music and let the rhythm inspire you to relax and recharge. Spread that Leo energy!

Experiment with Rosemary Essential Oil

While Leo's confidence and extroverted nature serve him well, it can also lead to stress. Combat burnout and practice self-care for your mind and body by embracing the power of rosemary essential oil.

This luxurious aroma appeals to Leo's zest for life, and also nurtures your body as you fight feelings of pressure. Try rubbing a few drops into your hands and feet when you need to reset your energy (be sure to dilute according to instructions, and use with caution if you have sensitive skin). If constant multitasking is leaving your brain spinning, massage your temples with a few drops of rosemary to improve your memory. Make it a ritual by dimming the lights and putting on some soft music—you'll soon find yourself ready for your next challenge.

Focus on the Flame

Fire signs are drawn to the sacred element inside them: the flame. From the blue center to the red-hot aura glowing outward, the flame calls you on an instinctual level. Use the power of fire to keep yourself balanced when you need it most. At times of high stress, find a quiet respite. Light a candle of your choosing and sit in front of it. Watch as the flame dances, softly flickering as it burns slowly. Take solace in the beauty of the flame before you, allowing the whole world to fall away around you. It is just you and the flame. Fix your gaze on the flame as it flares and sways, and try to quiet your mind as best as possible. If you find your mind wandering, don't worry. Gently return your focus to the flame in front of you. Repeat for as long as you wish or until the flame has extinguished.

Embrace Cooling Citrus in the Hot Weather

When the temperature rises, Leo's already fiery nature can hit a boiling point! But you can cool your jets *and* freshen your skin in one act! Try freshening up with orange blossom spray or lemon verbena body splash. Leo is drawn to bold, luxurious fragrances, and the strong, sunny colors appeal to Leo's affinity with the sun. Try keeping a bottle in the refrigerator, and misting your body when the heat gets too much. It will hydrate your skin, clear your mind, and reinvigorate you on a steamy day.

Find Your Passion

Discovering what kindles the passion inside you usually comes naturally for fire signs. After all you are full of strong emotions and big ideas, all of which drive your sense of knowing and well-being. Maybe it's a hobby that makes your heart sing, or a political cause, or a person. Hone in on those things and make them a prominent part of your life if they aren't already. Indulge in the passion you feel for them, and let it fill you with meaning and support. If you are unsure about what lights your fire, it's time to start learning about yourself. Try a new meal, make a new friend, read a new book. Your journey of self-discovery will lead you to your true passions.

Flirt

———————

Intimacy and sexual connection are key components in a relationship, especially for fire signs. You live to feel close to others and make your passion for them known in one way or another. When the mood strikes, unleash your inner flirt and have some fun with the person you are smitten with. Bat your eyes. Whisper sweet nothings. Tell them a corny joke. Let loose and show your unique personality.

Bring the Sun Indoors
with a Fruit Tree

While Leo would like to, basking in the sun isn't always an option! Harness the energy of your ruling planet by growing an orange or lemon tree indoors.

Caring for your tree can also be an act of self-care. After selecting the tree most appropriate for your living space, make its care a part of your daily routine—keep it watered and well lit, and keep an eye out for pests or brown/dead leaves.

Not only will you enjoy the vibrant energy of the tree as it grows, you'll also have a healthy, flavorful snack at your fingertips!

Combine Earth and Fire

S tone is one of the earth's most sacred elements, and with a touch of heat, it becomes the ultimate healing tool. You can benefit from the combination of these two elements by indulging in a hot-stone massage.

Fire signs are naturally active beings, often pushing their bodies to the limit with exercise and adventure. Take time to let your body relax and heal after strenuous activity, and why not do so with a soothing hot-stone massage? Not only do the stones connect with the primal fire inside you, but they expand your blood vessels, improving circulation and flushing your skin, all while relaxing sore muscles.

Add Glamour to Any Day

E ven confident Leo can lose a bit of sparkle in the day-to-day grind. When you're feeling particularly un-fierce, take small steps to add a bit of glamour back into your day.

Why not throw on your favorite pair of heels or your favorite item of clothing when you're watching *Netflix* on the couch? Wear your most luxurious robe while folding laundry. Use the holiday china to serve your Tuesday-night pizza delivery. Even when the workweek can zap your lust for life, put some celebration back in your self-care and make any day one to remember!

Try Spontaneity

When is the last time you did something completely on impulse? Hopefully not too long ago, because enthusiastic spontaneity is the ruling philosophy for all fire signs. Have you been feeling a little trapped lately? Stuck in a rut you just can't break free from? Don't ignore that little voice inside you urging you to do something a little out of your comfort zone. Being impulsive and spontaneous electrifies the fire sign's soul and feeds the energy within. Without it, you'll suffocate under the weight of predictability.

Build a Sacred Space

Leo benefits from any time spent basking in the glow of his ruling heavenly body, the Sun. Find the sunniest spot in your home and create a sanctuary of your very own—a place where you can practice self-care every day.

The time you spend in your sanctuary should empower you to lead with your natural generosity and warmth of spirit. If you find yourself veering toward brashness or arrogance, use your space as a place to re-center yourself. Harness the spirit of the sun, allowing you to maximize your potential and go about your day with a clear, focused mind.

Sit Like a Royal

Leo's home is his castle. Reign comfortably and confidently, in a large, comfy chair.

Every king needs a throne! Visit thrift stores and discount sites for a chair that resembles one fit for royalty. When you need to make important decisions or phone calls, sit upon your throne and be inspired by its power—and yours!

By adapting a king- or queen-like state of mind, you'll channel regal confidence and authority. When you need solace or rest, your throne can be a place for comfort and respite. While it may feel like an extravagance, the benefits of your special chair will far outweigh the cost.

Enjoy a Laugh

When you're in need of emotional release, turn to your favorite laugh-out-loud comedy. It may seem counterintuitive, but a funny movie is actually one of the best ways a fire sign can let go of any nasty emotions that have been building up over time. You have so much passion swirling inside you that you need a positive way to let it all out. If you have a favorite comedy, turn it on—or if you want to try something new, check out what's playing at your local theater. Need more of a reason to laugh? Not only does laughter help reduce stress hormones in your body, it also helps increase immune cells and releases endorphins, the body's feel-good chemical. Win-win!

Look to the Stars
(for Interior-Decorating Advice)

———————

An important aspect of self-care is creating an environment that is both welcoming and inviting. And since Leo is the sign of drama, perhaps you'd enjoy bringing that flair into your home by welcoming the heavens into your abode with gold star decorations.

Put a gold star on your front door to greet your guests with sparkle. Add a conversation piece to your living room by charting a Leo constellation on the wall. Invite some drama into the bedroom by putting stars over your bed. Whatever you fancy, this touch of sparkle will add a Leo-inspired spin to your home.

Make a List

F ire signs often have a lot of great ideas and like to
  start a variety of projects when inspiration strikes.
It's just part of the territory—you are naturally creative and dream big. The hurdle is completing these
projects.

Take a survey of your life and make note of different projects or plans that are sitting around half-
finished. Make a list of the tasks you want to complete
and when you want to complete them by. You can be
as specific or as vague as you want.

Maybe that wine rack you are building doesn't
need to be finished for another year or so, or maybe
you want to show off your favorite bottles by next
month. The ultimate goal is committing to expecta-
tions and following through on your plans. And just
imagine how much better you'll feel once you've
checked off a few of those projects from your list.

Burn, Baby, Burn

Fire is cathartic for fire signs. It can cleanse and purify your energy, and helps you let go of emotional burdens. From destruction comes regrowth, better and stronger than before.

Use the natural destruction inherent with fire to your advantage. Write down your feelings on a few pieces of paper. Light a candle and place it in a fire-safe bowl or in the sink. Carefully hold each piece of paper to the flame and allow it to catch fire. Watch as fire consumes your words and emotions. Drop the piece of paper into the sink or bowl to continue burning. As each emotion goes up in flames, feel the weight on your heart lessen. You are free, ready to rise from the ashes more resilient and determined.

Sleep It Off

A good night's sleep can be transformative, but unfortunately, fire signs often have a hard time getting enough sleep. As a fire sign, you naturally need less sleep than others, but that doesn't mean you are invincible. With all the activity you do every day, you need your rest.

Creating a good sleep routine is key. Take note of how you usually get ready for bed. Do you already have a routine, or does it change from night to night? Do you have a specific bedtime you shoot for, or do you stay up until different times depending on your mood?

To help stabilize your sleep schedule, try implementing a few easy, enjoyable activities you can do right before bed, anything from reading for a few minutes before closing your eyes to taking a long bath, or even meditating. Aim to get into bed at around the same time every night. Fire signs love spontaneity, but when it comes to good sleep hygiene, predictability is paramount.

Embrace the Power of Mirrors

———

Leo is the most aware of his image sign of the zodiac, and often needs to see random glimpses of himself. Feed your desire for attention by placing mirrors in a variety of places in your home. Hang a sunburst mirror center stage in the living room over the sofa. Decorate with mirrors of all sizes—maybe even a collage of mirrors on one wall?

Once you are happy with the arrangement, be sure to keep your mirrors clean. It will make your self-image sparkle.

Avoid Burnout

With all the complicated emotions you hold onto as a fire sign, it can sometimes be helpful to seek out a professional therapist to work through your thoughts. Talking to a professional is often a therapeutic experience and can promote overall wellness in your life. Fire signs are prone to emotional fatigue and burnout because their emotions run intensely for extended periods of time. It can drain your system to keep them bottled up. Eventually, you'll run out of gas. Turning to a trained professional who can help you understand and sort your stressors can save your emotional well-being and give you a healthy outlet to better yourself.

Change It Up

Predictability is the fire sign's ultimate enemy. How do you avoid getting stuck in the same humdrum pattern? Change things up. Start in your home, where you spend the majority of your time and where you feel the most comfortable.

To get the winds of change blowing, open your windows (if you can) and move your furniture around into different arrangements in all of your major spaces. This could mean moving your bed from one wall to the other or changing which direction your couch faces. It could also mean doing something as small as adding a piece of furniture to a room. Whatever feels right to you! Sometimes just changing your perspective can make all the difference in the world.

Make Your Home a Castle

Although Louis XIV was a Virgo, he was known as the Sun King. He was big into fashion, décor, and culture. If you're looking to inject some drama and fashion into your home, look to Versailles for inspiration.

Choose a canopy bed for the bedroom. Celebrate your regal nature by introducing royal accents into your home décor. Drape lush, velvety fabrics over your furniture and window treatments. While the exterior world can make all of us feel like lowly servants, a Leo can feel like royalty in his home fit for a king.

Take Care of Your Mane

A lion's mane is a point of pride—and the same should be true for Leo. An important part of self-care is feeling good about yourself, so if you need a boost, indulge yourself by cleaning out your old, expired, and no-good hair products in your cabinets, and make room for the new and improved!

New shampoo, conditioners, and vitamin-enriched hair products will keep Leo's mane shining. When you have time, treat yourself to a hair mask, Moroccan oil, or hot-oil treatment. Grooming shouldn't be tiresome—it can be an indulgent, spa-like experience. So light a candle, put on your favorite robe, and fluff some towels in the dryer so you have a warm towel after you get out of the bath or shower to create your own at-home spa.

Let There Be Light

———————————

During the winter months it's easy for vitamin D levels to plummet. What's a sun-loving Leo to do without daily access to the sun? Consider purchasing a good light box for the winter months to charge up Leo's solar battery.

Widely available online, these "happy lights" provide safe, natural light therapy that triggers our hormones and neurotransmitters, greatly affecting our mood. Leo will enjoy having some daily time "in the sun," and you can create a self-care ritual by making it a part of your daily morning routine in the months when sun is hard to come by.

Streamline Your Space

———————————

Clutter can do more than just cause a mess in your home. It can overwhelm your mind and make you feel trapped. Fire signs love big spaces with a lot of room to move around. If you find that you are feeling claustrophobic in your own living space, it might be time to streamline your belongings.

Start by going through your closets and cabinets and throw out anything you don't need. Next, move on to your furniture. Many fire signs find the minimalist design aesthetic a pleasing choice. Look for furniture that does double duty, like a combination desk and dining table. The most important thing is to give yourself space to feel free.

Try Cat Pose

In addition to the heart and back, Leo's ruler, the Sun, has always been associated with the spine. Keep your spine flexible with yoga—particularly Cat Pose, which is an effective, gentle way to warm up your spine.

The next time you feel a bit stiff, take a moment at work or home to take care of your spinal column. Using your favorite yoga app, book, or website, follow the simple instructions for Cat Pose, being sure to keep your knees directly below your hips and wrists. You may also want to complement Cat Pose on your exhales with Cow Pose on your inhales for a gentle vinyasa.

Follow Your Intuition

Your intuition is invaluable when it comes to decision-making. Fire signs often move from one idea to the next rather quickly, but your gut reaction to an idea can help inform whether you should pursue it or not. You don't have the time to sit and weigh the pros and cons, using your mind to decide. You use your heart and that feeling pulsing inside either urging you forward or calling out warnings to stop. Listen to that voice. It tells the most primal truths about your journey as a person, and its only purpose is to help you navigate through life's confusing moments.

Still aren't sure what your intuition is telling you? Sometimes, it can even be a physical feeling. Do you get a warm rush in your veins when you think of something? Or is it more of a stomachache? Our bodies have different ways of speaking to us. Listen for yours.

Give Fencing a Try

Feed Leo's desire for competition and drama with fencing!

Known as the fashionable sport of the aristocracy throughout the ages, fencing is one of the original Olympic sports. Today, it is recognized as an invigorating combination of physical and mental exercise. You can serve your need for both physical and mental self-care by trying it out.

It can be an incredibly social sport as well. Look for local fencing clubs who welcome new and learning members, and ask how you might get involved. Pay particular attention to protecting your heart during this stimulating and challenging sport.

Don't Test Your Limits

Fire signs have a tendency to overexert themselves, physically and emotionally. Because of this it's important to recognize your limits, and to try not to push them too much. If you find you have a propensity for going too far emotionally, it might be time to create a list of warning signs that you can flag for yourself. When you see those warning signs popping up in your thought pattern and behavior, or if you feel yourself getting too stressed and overwhelmed, schedule a self-care activity to help find equilibrium once again. It can be as simple as taking a bath or visiting an old friend.

If you push yourself athletically, always give your body time to recuperate. While fire signs always want to go farther and be better physically, not allowing your body to rest after physical exertion can increase your risk for serious injury. Don't let your fire burn too bright—you are your own best advocate for balance and well-being.

Hone Your Cat-Like Reflexes

Thanks to Leo's alignment with the lion, he enjoys cat-like reflexes. Hone these skills and practice physical self-care at the same time by trying a martial art.

Aikido and Tai Chi are elegant and rhythmic martial art practices. Aikido loosely translates to "the way of the harmonious spirit," and is a wonderful way to honor both your physical and spiritual health. While the focus of aikido is grappling and attacking, it also encourages controlled relaxation, flexibility, and endurance.

Tai Chi is a defense-based training, often practiced for the pursuit of longevity. While it is a martial art, some forms of the training are known for being practiced with very slow movements.

Classes for both are offered in many gyms and recreation centers, and provide a nice opportunity for social interaction.

Embrace H$_2$O

Water and fire are opposites. And while water can extinguish fire, those born as fire signs need water to keep them thriving and succeeding. With all the strenuous activities you do as a fire sign, don't forget to keep hydrated. It can be easy to forget to stop and drink water when you are focused on achieving a physical goal. Make it a priority to drink the recommended number of ounces of water a day, and more if you are engaging in demanding physical workouts. Remember that water will not smother the flame burning inside of you.

Stay Active in the Winter Months

Leo's affinity for the sun can make it tempting to hibernate in the colder months. Fight the urge and get outside, even when the mercury drops! Doing so will get you some much-needed sun during the winter months.

Braving the cold can also feed your sense of adventure. Why not try figure skating, snowboarding, skiing, or even sledding? Honor your childlike side by building a snowman or having a snowball fight with friends. You can get exercise, relieve stress, and enjoy the fresh air—a well-rounded act of self-care.

Beat the Heat

Balance can be the key to a happy life. As a fire sign, you must learn to offset your heat and passion with coolness. Begin with how you nourish your body. If it feels like your inner fire is burning too hot, put away the spices and try to balance the heat by eating cooling foods. Turn to foods such as watermelon, cucumber, and yogurt, and if you are feeling really indulgent, ice cream. The cool contrast will help keep your inner fire from burning out of control.

Stand Tall

Since Leo rules the spine, posture is of utmost importance. Be mindful, and be sure to sit and stand up straight.

Not only does good posture help to boost your confidence, it's also important for your physical self-care. Good posture helps to keep your bones and joints in proper alignment, decreases stress on ligaments, and prevents the spine from adjusting to unnatural positions.

Whether your work requires you to sit for long periods of time or you catch yourself slouching when you grow fatigued, make an effort to maintain awareness of how you are supporting your back, neck, and head. You'll find that by being mindful of how you are sitting or standing, you will naturally sit up taller and prouder. Adopt the posture of royalty!

Try the Ancient Power of Hot Yoga

Bikram yoga is a form of yoga done in an environment where the temperature is about 104°F. Heat is a vital element of this exercise. Practicing yoga in a heated room is a great way to potentially increase your metabolism and your heart rate, which in turn allows your blood vessels to expand and your muscles to become more flexible.

This form of hot yoga is perfect for fire signs. Fire signs feed off of the heat around them, and use it to find equilibrium and balance. Look for hot yoga classes near you to challenge yourself and your body. If you've never tried a hot yoga class before, be sure to hydrate your body beforehand and to bring a small towel with you to class. Get ready to sweat!

Accessorize

Your Leo nature means you favor bold colors and outfits that command attention. Sometimes, though, professional obligations or other circumstances require more formal or staid looks. In these circumstances maintain formality but add a touch of drama with colorful scarves, jewelry, gloves, ties, or handbags.

Keep an eye out for inexpensive, one-of-a-kind accessories in thrift shops and on vintage-clothing websites. Whether multicolored or sparkly, the more eye-catching, the better!

These fun accessories allow you to make a statement and express yourself no matter what the occasion. Let your lion roar, Leo!

Draw a Bath

As a fire sign you already have a special affinity to heat and its galvanizing power. But it is also a wonderful relaxation tool. Warm water can be incredibly soothing for a weary fire sign. If your mind is cluttered from the demands of day-to-day life, and your muscles are sore from all of the physical activities you do, climb into a warm bath and let the water alleviate your ailments.

You can even add a special bath bomb or bubbles to the bath to make it more relaxing. Go for scents like lavender, jasmine, or even rose to ease your mind. Adding Epsom salt to the warm water can help take the ache out of overused muscles. Add 1 cup of Epsom salt to the bath as the water runs and enjoy as the warm water soothes your body and soul.

Wear Your Heart on Your Wrist

———————————

L eading with your heart, Leo, create a piece of jewelry that combines history and beauty.

Beautiful and full of love, a charm bracelet (or leather cuff) is the perfect bauble for Leo. Find charms (or symbolic embellishments) that represent your interests and memories. Gold and rubies are favorites for Leo, with the gold representing bold beauty and the ruby being Leo's birthstone.

This wearable memento can be eye-catching and sentimental at once, inviting questions from curious friends and family that lead to walks down memory lane. Spend time to make your wrist accessory both attractive and meaningful, as Leo prefers.

Enlist in Boot Camp

B oot camp–style exercise classes are popular
fitness options for fire signs looking to add a
little heat to their typical workout regime. These boot
camps attract a wide variety of people, and the group
atmosphere can really ignite a spark for fire signs
who love a little friendly competition. You'll learn to
encourage others to push their physical limit, and
to push your own limit as well. The combination of
intense cardiovascular or strength-training exercises
with a supportive team dynamic can be a rewarding
experience for many fire signs. Make friends, build
muscle, and tone your heart, all at the same time.

Enjoy Fireside Chats

The fireplace is often the center of the home. It's where people gather together to keep warm and to share stories. As a fire sign, you have an innate connection to fireplaces—they feel comfortable to you, like old friends. If you have a fireplace in your home, make it the center of your space. Arrange seating around the fireplace so it becomes the focal point. Use it as often as you can to take advantage of your sacred connection to the fire it contains.

If you don't have a fireplace already, you can often buy a decorative, portable fireplace from many home goods stores. Just the look of fire dancing can pacify a stressed-out fire sign. If you can't have any sort of fireplace, decorative or not, in your home, look for a restaurant or bar nearby that has one and make that your new go-to spot for drinks, dinner, and cozy relaxation.

Go on a Digital Detox

Fire signs are always moving from one thing to the next. That's because they are ambitious and motivated, traits that can sometimes lead to some serious burnout if you aren't careful.

One way to purposefully give yourself a break from the fast pace of the world around you is to unplug digitally as often as possible. Try and put your phone or tablet away at the same time every night, approximately an hour before bedtime. This gives your mind time to unwind before sleep.

If you go on vacation, consider switching your phone on just once a day to check for urgent messages. At home, designate a basket for devices and ask that family members place their phones and tablets in it before time meant to be spent together. And when going to dinner with friends, focus on enjoying your food and company—not keeping one eye on your phone at all times.

Expand Your Jewelry Collection

Need a recharge? Look to your jewelry box! Amber jewelry, cat's eye, and tiger's eye are all sun-kissed stones ruled by Leo. Incorporate them into your collection, and wear them when you are looking for a quick hit of sun, or just to make a bold fashion statement!

Leo enjoys attention, and these conversation pieces are sure to attract the eye of friends and family. This small action will keep you feeling confident, looking your best, and feeding your desire for the sun—it's an indulgent yet doable act of self-care!

Give Yourself a Hand

What to do when you're craving some attention and praise, but aren't around other people? Give yourself a hand with an applause box!

Congratulate yourself frequently with this round of applause you control. Simply lift the lid and you'll be greeted with a warm applause. While it may seem silly, this simple act of self-care can boost your self-esteem and feed your confident nature. Use it to pump yourself up before a work presentation or first date, or to reward yourself for tackling a long-delayed chore around the house. No occasion is too small to celebrate. Take a bow, Leo!

Catch Some Rays

———————————

Spending time outside soaking up the sun can lift any fire sign's mood. Think of yourself as a solar panel. You need the sunlight to reenergize your soul when you are feeling depleted. Lucky for fire signs, sunlight can help increase your levels of serotonin—those feel-good chemicals in your brain—thus boosting your happy mood.

Take some time to bathe in the sun, letting the rays wash over you. Feel the warmth on your skin, and imagine the sunshine penetrating down into your heart, lighting you up on the inside. Bask in the warmth around you.

While sun exposure, at the right times and intensity, can be beneficial for anyone, too much sun can be dangerous, even if you are a fire sign. While you're recharging in the sun, always take the proper precautions, like wearing sunscreen and remembering to reapply.

Indulge in the Theater

Leo loves drama and spectacle. There is a perfect place to celebrate this love—the theater! Become a seasonal supporter of a local theater and go frequently. The music, costumes, and dramatic dialogue combine for an experience sure to feed your creative soul.

If your craving for attention extends to the spotlight, you might even consider auditioning for a part! If you'd rather, you could volunteer to help out backstage, or with costume and scenery prep. Whether in the audience, on the stage, or behind the curtains, the theater is a wonderful place to indulge in the creative aspect of self-care. Bravo, Leo!

Get Creative

Being creative comes naturally to fire signs. They are often temperamental and passionate, and need a healthy way to release the emotions inside of them. While many fire signs turn to physical activities like athletics to help control the blaze within, flexing your creative muscles can be just as beneficial. Try indulging in the creative arts as inspiration. Hobbies such as painting, pottery, coloring, writing, or even knitting or scrapbooking can fuel your creative spark. Get a friend to join you as well. There are tons of ways to let your creativity run free. The only limit is your own imagination.

Crown Yourself King!

———————————

I ndulge your inner king or queen—with a crown! While it may feel silly, a crown represents royalty. What better way to honor Leo's symbol, the Lion? Leo enjoys attention, and you're sure to spark conversation when wearing a crown or tiara. After all, royalty needs to be recognized.

Or perhaps you don your crown when you're feeling not-so-fabulous. While the lion is the well-known regal king of the jungle, you can use your crown to boost confidence and to lift yourself up—a true act of self-care.

Take a Trip

Fire signs are drawn to impulse and improvisation. If they don't feed their desire for adventure on a regular basis, fire signs can sometimes get cranky and start feeling stuck. To remedy this, cash in your airplane miles and take a last-minute trip to somewhere you've always wanted to visit. Even a last-minute weekend trip to another town nearby can satisfy a fire sign's need for fresh scenery. Your need to explore unfamiliar territory can lead you to great discoveries about yourself and the world around you. Don't let the fear of the unknown stop you. Be spontaneous!

Test Your Luck

———————————

Looking to enjoy an unusual night out? Try a casino! Leo is typically lucky with card games of chance, and the casino setting can be both social and dramatic.

Make the evening more special by adding some Leo flair to your outfit that night—a flashy evening gown or a sharp suit will make you the center of attention at the tables or slots.

Once you've gained some confidence, work your way over to the blackjack or poker tables—there you can show off your excellence at card games!

Get Physical

Making time for yourself can be difficult when you are a fire sign. You are always going, going, going, with very little downtime. There's always so much to do, and so little time to do it. Who wants to spend their free time going to the doctor? But, as a fire sign, it's important to make your health a priority. You tend to push yourself both physically and mentally, striving for the next success benchmark. Make sure you keep tabs on your health, and schedule an annual physical checkup with your doctor to make sure you are healthy and strong. Your wellness should never be put on the back burner.

Greet the Day

———————————

Whether you are an early bird or a night owl, as a fire sign you have a natural attraction to the sun. You are drawn to its power and heat, and can often generate strength from its rays. Don't ignore this special connection you have with the sun. Embrace its energy and start your day by going for a long morning walk. Beginning the day by communing with the element that speaks to you the most will help set the stage for a positive afternoon, evening, and night ahead.

Check In on Your Emotions

Your emotional health is often overlooked when you're a fire sign. You are constantly moving from one thing to the next, so you may not make time to take your emotional temperature. Fire signs also spend a lot of time supporting and entertaining others emotionally. You are the first to step up and help a friend in need, but that concern doesn't transfer to your own well-being. Check in with yourself as often as possible. Are you stressed? Tired? Overwhelmed? Make a list of what you are feeling. If any of those feelings intensify, take some time to practice self-care in whatever form that suits you best.

Take a Break from Social Media

Leo loves attention. And what easier way to receive this attention than some innocent posts on social media? Well, they may not be so innocent if you find yourself preoccupied with keeping up your appearance online, and if you equate your self-worth with how many likes and shares you receive.

Consider a social media detox. You could even try a social media challenge with your friends, daring each other to unplug from your favorite chosen social platform for a week—or more.

Love social media too much to unplug? Even just cutting down on social media use by a few minutes per day can help.

Just Say No

Fire signs are prone to saying yes to everything, almost to a fault. You tend to move from one activity to the next, accepting the latest invite and helping friends whenever they need. That's wonderful for everyone else, but it also means you burn both ends of your candle, until sometimes the only thing left is ashes. To help keep your fire from going out, practice saying no when you are feeling overextended. This may happen at work, with friends, with your family, or even to yourself. Prioritize your own needs over others. Know there is nothing wrong with taking time to stoke your own flame.

Embrace Your Childlike Nature

One of the greatest acts of emotional self-care is spending time with children: others' or your own. Leo has a natural affinity with the enthusiasm and charm of kids, and time spent with them can be a wonderful way to de-stress and have fun.

Leo and children alike enjoy being outside in the sun, so play a simple game of tag, go to a playground, or just go for a walk. Allow the kids to take the lead, and your eyes will be opened to their joy and appreciation for the simplest things life has to offer.

Strike a Work-Life Balance

As a fire sign, you have a passion to succeed in every aspect of your life. While this burning desire to achieve greatness powers your professional performance, it can also cause your work life to take over your whole life. It's important for your overall well-being that you keep your life inside the office balanced with your life outside the office. If you set boundaries between your professional and personal lives, you will be more productive at work and more fulfilled outside of it. You don't want to neglect your work responsibilities, but it's important to disconnect and recharge. By striking this work-life balance, you'll continue to succeed without burning out.

Keep Your Cool

Fire signs can be temperamental at times. It's not your fault. You are naturally feisty and passionate, both positive traits that make you loyal and hard-working. Sometimes, though, you can get a little too overheated. At that point it's important to take a step back before you lose your cool too much. One trick you can try is to count to five in your head, or out loud. An alternate option is to exhale first and then inhale and repeat three times. Either way, you'll give yourself a moment to curtail the strong emotions that are driving you. Practice tamping down the fire within you without letting it go out.

Host Regular Gatherings

———————

Leo loves to entertain. Show off your kingdom and spend time socializing with friends and family by hosting social occasions in your home.

Try a game night—a great chance to have some laughs and bask in the spotlight. A book club could be a great chance to spark discussion and meet new people. Or perhaps set up a regular dinner group— Leo loves showing off his culinary skills and dining with friends. Consider featuring ingredients such as almonds, basil, coconut, ginger, sunflower seeds, and arugula in your dishes. These flavors particularly appeal to Leo.

Enjoy the Sunset

———————

The sun is very symbolic for fire signs. Its energy sustains and comforts you, so it's no surprise that watching the sun set after a long day can help you relax and find peace. Find a local spot with a great view if you can, and settle in for a show. Find solace in watching the different colors that emanate across the sky as the sun dips below the horizon: from bright orange, to light pink, soft periwinkle, to, finally, a deep blue. Let the phases of its descent remind you that with every ending comes a beginning. The sun goes down, and the sun comes up.

Celebrate Anything with Champagne

L eo loves adding a pop of drama and excitement to any old day. What better way to do so than to pop a bottle of champagne?

Don't just reserve the bubbly for special occasions—add some excitement to brunch, a touch of class to happy hour, and some fizzy fun to girls' (or boys') night out. By making these small moments occasions to remember, you're taking care to mark life's small joys, and to be more present in the moment—a great way to focus on your emotional self-care.

Visualize the Sun

When you need a mental break but can't get away, try using visualization exercises. Since Leo thrives on the sun's energy, it can provide a great focus point for your practice.

Whether you're working or not, take a moment to clear your head. Then, if you're able, close your eyes and picture the golden warmth of the sun. Imagine the feel of its comforting heat on your skin, and picture the glow of the sun's light reflecting off water. Taking deep, calming breaths during your visualization, continue your exercise until you feel ready to return to your day. It's a small yet effective moment for spiritual self-care.

Go for a Ride

———————————

S atisfy your fiery sense of adventure with a spontaneous mini-road trip. Take the back roads, avoid the highways, and make this a leisurely trip to clear your mind, ease your spirit, and reignite your wanderlust. You don't necessarily need to have a final destination in mind; just embrace the journey and the open road. As you're driving, you can sing along to your favorite playlist or put on a podcast or audiobook. Take the time alone in your car to enjoy yourself and your surroundings. It does not need to be a lengthy drive in order to experience its benefits—you just need to relax and enjoy the ride.

Let the Music Move You

Nothing gets Leo moving like music with a beat. When you're looking for some tunes to perk up your day or get the evening started, try samba, merengue, or Latin ballroom—all are sure to get the Lion's toes tapping.

Since Leo is the "look at me" sign, he particularly enjoys music he can be a part of, even in subtle ways. Music that is easy to sing along to or fun to dance to is at the top of Leo's playlist. If you're not familiar with samba, merengue, or Latin ballroom, look online for suggestions for artists and songs to listen to. Or take it one step further and consider signing up for a dance class, or research places to go out dancing for the evening. You'll feel like you're part of the show!

Spice It Up

Just as he enjoys drama in every other aspect of his life, Leo likes cuisine with dramatic tastes. While you may not have the time to make intricately prepared meals every day, there are some easy ways to add some drama to your meals!

In the morning try making your scrambled eggs with plain yogurt instead of milk—it will give them a tangy flavor. If you like heat, add a dash of hot sauce.

For lunch add dried fruit and seeds to your salad, or fresh herbs and exotic cheeses to liven up your sandwich.

For dinner use cinnamon to flavor meat dishes—this spice will add a rich, bold taste to your meals. Eat up, Leo!

Get Some Fresh Air

———————————

Oxygen feeds fire, so when you feel your spark starting to dim, take 10 minutes to go outside and breathe in the fresh air. Whether you're at work or at home, it's the perfect way to take some time for yourself and recharge. As you're enjoying the fresh air, allow yourself to live in that moment. Take a deep, meaningful breath in through your nose, hold for 5 seconds, and breathe out through your mouth. Feel the air fill your lungs and circulate through your body. This simple mindful breathing exercise feeds your internal flame, calms your mind, and reenergizes your spirit.

Forgive Yourself

As a fire sign, it's easy to go from passionate to incensed. Usually, these feelings are reserved for people who aren't able to keep up with your fiery spirit. However, what happens when you are the one you're upset with? If you've done something that's created your own mental hang-up, you need to extinguish those feelings sooner rather than later. You don't want to be your own worst enemy. While it's important to keep yourself accountable, you also need to be able to forgive yourself for any missteps or mistakes you've made. Release those feelings that have been burning you up inside and channel your energy into positive thoughts and actions.

Write Out Your Thoughts

Fire signs are known for following their gut instincts, but with all the background noise buzzing around you, it can be hard to hone in on what your gut is saying. Try a stream-of-consciousness writing exercise to amplify your inner monologue. First, clear your mind. Next, think about something you feel you need guidance on: anything from a career question, to relationships, to personal development. Then just start writing. Don't think too much about what you are writing; just allow the words to flow. Write for as long as you want. In the end you may find the answer you were looking for all along buried within your words.

Turn to Turmeric

Take a moment for health—and flavor—by incorporating turmeric into your diet.

Turmeric has wonderful anti-inflammatory properties, and its golden, sun-like color particularly appeals to Leo. Work it into your diet for an easy yet effective act of self-care.

Try sprinkling turmeric on rice or vegetables. Rub it into poultry and meat before cooking, or, if you really love the flavor, make yourself a turmeric smoothie. Preparing and drinking this healthy, flavorful beverage can easily become part of your morning routine, a self-care ritual that will start your day off on the healthy foot.

Don't Skimp on the SPF

Just because fire signs have a unique connection to the sun doesn't mean they still can't get burned by its power. Given the amount of time you spend outside keeping active, make sure to wear sunscreen and/or protect your skin with UV-blocking clothing. Hats are particularly important, as is reapplying sunscreen every hour or so when you are in the sun. If you've already spent too much time outside and gotten burned, a bottle of aloe vera gel can soothe the sting and help your skin heal more quickly.

Inspire Others

You are lucky to have such a powerful flame burning inside you. Fire signs may forget that not everyone possesses their same ambition and fervor. Use your natural fire for good and inspire someone else in your life.

Try sending a friend or a loved one a card of encouragement. The small gesture can help light a fire under them and give them the strength to take a risk. If sending a card isn't your cup of tea, a text, email, or phone call can offer the same sentiment. The goal is to reach out and share your own fire with someone else who needs it.

Make It Extra-Virgin

Since Leo rules the heart, it is extra important that he takes care of his ticker. An easy way to take care of your heart? Cook with extra-virgin olive oil!

Olive oil is an effective way to combat heart disease, thanks to its superpowered monounsaturated fat content. It also contains powerful antioxidants.

While it can be hard to find time to exercise, odds are, you cook or eat a meal every day that, with simple adjustments, can be given a heart-healthy makeover with the addition of extra-virgin olive oil. To your health, Leo!

Let It Go

Holding on to negative emotions can do long-term damage to your well-being. Because of how passionate you can be as a fire sign, you may find you let resentment or other destructive feelings boil inside you. Let those feelings go. Don't allow them to fester and build inside of you until they get to an unmanageable point. Release any grudges you have against a person who has wronged you and forgive them for their wrongdoing. Once you let these emotions loose into the universe, you'll begin to heal and open up to more positivity and light.

Take a Risk

You already know that, as a fire sign, you have great instincts, but you may struggle with acting on them. Trust your gut and take a risk. Ask someone out on a date, apply for a new job, or make a large purchase that you've been eyeing for a while. Do something risky for yourself. It's easy to tell yourself "I'll do it later" or "It's not the right time." There's no time like the present. It might seem scary when you are in the moment, but big risks often mean big rewards. Tap into that passion churning inside you and take a leap of faith.

Have a Cup of Chamomile

Soothe your system in the evening by sipping tea made from Leo's herb: chamomile. Medicinally, chamomile can have anti-inflammatory properties and aid in digestion. On an astrological and spiritual level, chamomile is ruled by the Sun, the governing celestial body for Leo. The flowers are solar yellow, and it can have a wonderful calming effect for Leo.

Rather than buying your tea in a store, consider making your own with fresh chamomile flowers (often found at health food stores or farmers' markets; if you suffer from plant allergies or are on medication, check with your doctor before taking chamomile).

Heat 8 ounces of water in your tea kettle or pot. Remove the stems from the flowers, until you have 3–4 tablespoons of chamomile. If you like mint, you may add a fresh sprig. When the water has boiled, pour over the flowers and mint. Steep for 5 minutes (or more, if you like a stronger flavor). Pour the liquid through a fine strainer into a teacup, and enjoy.

Treat Yourself to a Head Massage

If a professional masseuse is out of your budget, instead get a haircut (complete with wash and scalp massage) or ask a loved one to brush your hair.

Just as his mane is the lion's source of pride and joy, so too is Leo's hair. Anything that stimulates the hair follicles makes Leo happy because it contributes to healthy, luxurious hair. While your scalp and hair follicles are stimulated, you can relax and enjoy the feeling of someone massaging your head. De-stressing and beautifying—a true dual act of self-care!

Become a Gamer

Fire signs are competitive when it comes to just about anything. Even the most mundane of tasks can become a game for you, one that you absolutely must win. To feed your competitive spirit in a healthy manner, try playing a board game. You're already used to being active outside, taking on one athletic challenge and then the next. Now train your mind. There are so many options to help you start flexing your brain muscles, from classic games like Monopoly and Scrabble to team games like charades, and even strategy and role-playing games. Buy a few and then have your friends over for a good old-fashioned game night!

Let the Sunshine In

_____

Even the king has to work every once in a while.
When you're stuck indoors working, you don't
have to miss the light of the sun. Try replacing the
light bulbs in your work space with full spectrum light
bulbs. These bulbs cover all wavelengths that are use-
ful to plant or animal life. In short, they imitate Leo's
ruler, the Sun.

While nothing can replicate the feeling of being
outside in the warming sunshine, full spectrum light
bulbs are the next best thing. While these bulbs are
slightly more expensive than their standard counter-
parts, your self-care is worth every penny.

Heal Your Bruised Ego

Self-confidence is a wonderful trait of Leo's. However, pride can easily turn into arrogance, which can be one of Leo's less-attractive qualities.

If a friend or family member has injured your pride, consider forgiveness. Leo's great lesson is to overcome inflexible pride. Forgiving someone who has done you wrong, or who you have perceived as doing you wrong, will lift an emotional weight. Consider this an act of emotional self-care as holding a grudge is unhealthy for you, and serves no purpose.

After you have cleared the air, take care not to end up in the same situation in the future. Remember that self-confidence is very good; cocky pride will only get you in trouble.

Seek Your Fire Totem

Your fire is unique to you. To remind yourself of this, seek out a personal totem that symbolizes your fire and flame that you can keep with you at all times. A totem is a sacred object that serves as an emblem for a group of people. In your case this totem will symbolize your connection to the fire burning within. It could be a piece of jewelry such as a bracelet, necklace, cuff, or amulet, or even a small desk trinket that you can keep by your side at work. There's no right or wrong when it comes to choosing your totem. Focus on something that calls to you and makes you feel brave and powerful when it is in your presence.

Re-Examine Yourself

At times Leo can be devoted to the image of himself rather than the substance. Could you be overlooking your genuine qualities? Look within and see.

Choose a quiet moment when you have time to focus. Write down what you believe to be your best qualities. Do not focus on superficial qualities, such as your physical appearance, strength at a particular sport, or role as the life of the party. Rather, think about the qualities you have that can be used for good. Do you have a generous spirit? Are you a wonderful listener? Can you make other people comfortable in otherwise awkward situations? Consider if you are using your genuine qualities to the best of your ability. By focusing on them, you are more likely to do so. Not only will you be taking care of yourself, but you will be taking care of others as well.

Make a Game of It

Fire signs can get bored easily. They are drawn to adventure and spontaneity, so the last thing they want is to get stuck in a pattern of tedium. Unfortunately, everyone has responsibilities they would rather not do, but how you react to those responsibilities is your choice. Tap into your fun-loving nature and make things more playful. Whether it's at work or around the house, turn your chores and responsibilities into a game. Even something as mundane as vacuuming the living room becomes a game when you set a timer for yourself. It makes things fun, feeds your competitive nature, and gets finished what needs to be done. In the end, changing how you think about a task can change how you complete it.

Pick Up a New Hobby

With such a strong personality, Leo's interests vary greatly. One thing is for sure, though—Leo does best when he keeps his mental and physical acuity sharp, so if you're lacking in hobbies at the moment, seek out a new one, or revisit an old one.

Since Leo loves being the center of attention, you may want to consider the dramatic or other creative arts. Audition with a local theater group, join a choir, or enter a piece in an art competition. Your creative juices will flow, and you'll be able to indulge your love of the limelight.

At the other end of the spectrum, Leo's abundance of energy makes physical-based hobbies a nice fit. Consider adventure sports, or physical activities that combine your love of attention and exercise, such as ice skating or ballroom dancing.

Go Out Dancing

If you want drama, rhythm, and physical release, a night out dancing is the perfect way for Leo to let off some steam.

Be the star of the dance floor and let loose with friends or family. Whether you're a trained dancer or just want to have fun, an evening spent dancing is a perfect activity for Leo. Consider dressing the part by picking an outfit that gives a nod to the type of music you'll be dancing to. If you're in the mood, sip some bubbly before hitting the floor to add a celebratory feel.

No matter the occasion, a night out dancing is always time well spent!

Smile

Smiling can change how you see the world, and how the world sees you. In fact, some studies suggest that the physical act of smiling can trick your brain into being happy even when you are in a bad mood. As a fire sign, you have so much love and happiness inside you—let it shine through and catch on like wildfire. Make a deal with yourself to smile at one stranger a day. Because your happy energy is contagious as a fire sign, this small act of kindness could do wonders for boosting someone's mood.

Try Open Mic Night

———————

Leo loves to be a star—taking part in an open mic night is a great way to express creativity! Get a few friends and head out to a local coffee shop or bar to take the stage. If you can't find an open mic night near you, create your own!

Invite friends and family over for a night to enjoy your talents. In addition to basking in the limelight, you can socialize, and, as a natural leader, encourage your more timid friends to show off their talents. It's a time to have fun, feed your creative side, and support your loved ones.

Splurge on the Royal Treatment

S tressed out and need some royal pampering?
Head to the spa, Leo!

A luxurious spa day may be the closest we can get
to being treated like kings and queens. Whether you
decide to get a manicure and pedicure, facial, or hot-
stone massage, treat yourself by going to a spa where
you feel comfortable and pampered.

Perhaps the most indulgent of treatments? The
full-body massage. Ask your masseuse to let you pick
out a scented oil, and give feedback early on so that
he or she applies the level of pressure you're most
comfortable with.

If a spa day isn't in the cards, have a close friend
over so you can give each other scalp and hand mas-
sages, pedicures, and facials (or just treat yourself to
an at-home treatment). The point is to indulge your
inner royal lion!

Treat Yourself

_____

You spend a lot of time entertaining those around you. The energy you have as a fire sign is infectious, so it's no wonder that people are drawn to you. You also love making people smile and laugh—it comes naturally and boosts your mood. Despite your penchant for entertaining, it's important to give yourself a break every once in a while. Alone time can be just as beneficial as time spent with large groups. Take yourself out to dinner once a month as a treat. To keep things lively, sit at the bar and people watch. Keep yourself open to new conversation with other bar patrons. Allowing your server to wait on you for once will help rejuvenate your spirit.

Lay Out in the Sun

A ny time you're craving an indulgent, relaxing, and inexpensive act of self-care, look no farther than your own backyard.

Break out the sunscreen and towel, and lay out in the sun. The Sun is Leo's ruling heavenly body, and reflects the core of Leo's being. Leo's passion for life and confidence comes from the sun, and he craves and draws power from it.

While lying in the sun can be emotionally fortifying, it can also be incredibly physically relaxing. So unwind and soak up the energizing rays!

Try a Fire Craft

Fuel your creative spark by taking up a craft that is powered by fire. While regular crafting such as painting, drawing, and sculpting are all wonderful ways to unwind and explore your artistic side, as a fire sign you crave something with a little more heat. Try pottery making, glassblowing, or woodburning to satiate your appetite. Your innate connection to fire will only deepen your creative reach and encourage your imagination. Find inspiration in how the heat transforms different materials—how it hardens clay, melts glass, and singes wood. Honor the power of fire through the creative process.

Spend Time with Your Friends

———————————

Hanging out with friends is a great act of self-care regardless of your astrological sign. It's a wonderful way to release stress, have some laughs, and enjoy yourself. But for Leo, time with friends is even more meaningful. Two of Leo's best qualities are loyalty and generosity of spirit. So why not throw your friends a special party to show them how much you appreciate them?

Whether an intimate dinner, a game night, or a raucous weekend party complete with high spirits and dancing, taking time to show your friends how much you care for them is a special gift for them—and for you!

Share Your Knowledge

Sharing expertise and teaching others are core Leo values. Tap into these important qualities, and teach a friend, family member, or coworker a skill to enrich his or her life.

Whether the skill is artistic and crafty, practical, physical, or mental, there is value in sharing. And if you think you don't have a talent to share, think again. Not all skill sets are glamorous or difficult to master. If you have a secret for removing stains, a knack of finding vintage handbags, or the recipe for the best smoothie to make for a postworkout recovery, share these tips with someone who could benefit. Share that Leo brainpower!

Binge a New Show

There's nothing quite like snuggling up on the couch in front of your TV (or laptop) after a long day. As a fire sign, you've probably been jumping from one activity to the next, trying to keep active and keep yourself moving. But there's nothing wrong with slowing down for a bit. Binge-watching a new show can be the perfect break you need from your hectic schedule. Make a night of it, and burn through every episode you can find. Make a bowl of popcorn, open a bottle of wine, and kick off your shoes. Let yourself become obsessed with knowing what happens next.

Adopt a Lion

Perhaps the most iconic astrological symbol, the Lion is the embodiment of all things Leo. And while this regal animal is the king of the jungle, the species is considered vulnerable to the possibility of extinction, and its population continues to decline. Lend a hand to your astrological brother and consider adopting a lion.

Through organizations such as the World Wildlife Fund, you can contribute to the care of lions by symbolically adopting a lion in the wild. You'll help to support those people committed to protecting the species, and make a positive contribution to global conservation efforts. If you have a loved one who is also a Leo, consider gifting him or her the adoption of a lion—a thoughtful and particularly meaningful gift for a fellow member of your astrological pride.

Go Nuts

Not only does Leo represent the heart, it also rules over this important organ. When Leo falls ill, many times it is due to diseases or ailments of the heart. While a heart-healthy diet and cardio exercise are important to consider at all times, consider taking your physical self-care to the next level by munching on walnuts and almonds.

While most nuts are generally healthy, walnuts and almonds are heart-health superstars. Walnuts contain high amounts of omega-3 fatty acids, and almonds are packed with healthy monounsaturated fats. Enjoy a delicious snack and take care of your heart with these healthy nuts!

Become More Patient

Fire signs have so many wonderful personality traits. Your level of loyalty, ambition, and passion is something to be envied. But you also have some unfavorable traits that you can work on. For example, your fieriness can often be interpreted by others as impatience. As a fire sign, your emotions tend to escalate very quickly, and your intensity can sometimes get the best of you.

Patience is a skill that often takes practice. Make it a personal goal to become more patient with others, situations, and yourself. When you feel that you are losing your patience, take a few deep breaths to de-escalate your emotions before they go too far. You have the power to control how you react to what you are feeling inside.

Lounge Like Majesty

After the stress of the day leaves you craving comfort and indulgence, wouldn't it be nice to retreat to the luxury of a plush, cozy bathrobe and inviting slippers?

While these particular wardrobe items won't see beyond the front door of your home, they're worth investing in. Few items can be both glamorous and comfortable like a lush robe! Treat yourself to a soothing bath and then wrap yourself in your robe, or simply put it on at the end of the day when you're longing to feel spoiled. After you slide into your slippers and put up your feet, you can relax like a royal!

Start an Idea Book

Fire signs are known for their creativity and great ideas. Don't risk letting those good ideas slip away by not taking the time to write them down. Consider buying an idea journal where you can keep track of all the cool things that you come up with on a daily basis. Similar to a dream journal, an idea journal is the perfect place to house your million-dollar thoughts. These journals are specifically created to help you tease out and capture your next great idea, and many even have prompts to inspire and challenge you. Never forget another genius idea again!

Don't Forget about You

While Leo often feels most comfortable in the limelight, being the center of attention can be draining. When you're beginning to feel stressed or drained, be sure to take some time for yourself.

Whether it's a day without leaving the house or a lunch break spent reading a book on your own, solo time is important when Leo needs to recharge. Afterward, you can rejoin your day with a renewed sense of energy.

Additionally, you may want to take some time to reflect on what preceded you feeling such a way so that you can avoid feeling emotionally, mentally, and physically drained in the future.

Fight for Your Rights

Use your passion to change the world. Fire signs have a lot of strong opinions and personal beliefs. Identify those causes that mean the most to you and put all of your energy into fighting for them. Whether it's environmental issues, animal welfare, women's and LGBTQ+ rights, veterans' affairs, or anything else that lights your fire, know that you can make a difference just by showing up and being present. Start by joining a social media group that gives updates about organized protests near you. Volunteer on weekends at local shelters. Make signs for rallies. Whatever it takes. Fight for what you believe, and inspire and motivate others to do the same.

Enjoy Some Retail Therapy

Leo loves luxurious fashions and home decorations. The next time you need a pick-me-up, why not hit the stores and look for your next great find?

Leo enjoys showing off, so be sure to punctuate your wardrobe with glitzy pieces that can dress up your wardrobe and reflect your personality. When you're shopping for your home, look for unique pieces that reflect your sense of self and align with the environment you want to create. Your home should be an extension of yourself so that you can truly relax and rejuvenate when you return there at the end of the day.

Not only should the act of shopping be an act of self-care, but you should also keep in mind how your purchases will contribute to your life.

Try a Rose Mist

S elf-care may not come easy to a fire sign. You are used to caring for others, and can sometimes forget to tend your own fire. Before you know it, your flame is burning out of control. A refreshing mist is a quick and easy way to balance the fire inside you, and to give yourself a few moments of self-care.

Rosewater is especially therapeutic for irritated skin. Rosewater is a hydrating blend made by steeping rose petals in water. Spritz it over clean skin and breathe in the calming scent of roses. Take a moment to pause and enjoy the sensations around you.

While you can find rosewater in many grocery and health stores, you can also make your own. First, boil a large pot of water, and remove the petals from a few roses. Add the petals to the water, and allow to simmer over medium-high heat for 20–30 minutes, or until the petals have lost the majority of their color. Allow to cool, strain the petals, and add the water to a clean spray bottle.

Repeat the Mantra, "I Will"

At his best Leo is passionate and caring, with a flair for the dramatic. At his worst Leo can be self-centered and aggressive. If you feel yourself drifting toward selfish behavior, keep yourself in check by repeating the mantra "I will."

When you focus on this phrase, think about what you can and will do to turn your thinking and behavior from self-centered to self-confident. Remind yourself of how you can share your gifts with your loved ones, and how you benefit from the help and love of others.

Have a Solo Dance Party

B reak out your dancing shoes and turn on your favorite jam. It's time for a solo dance party! Dancing is a wonderful way for fire signs to expel built-up energy that they haven't been able to let go of yet. It gets your heart pumping and your endorphins flowing. Plus, it's just plain fun. Let loose and really go for it. There's no one there to judge your dance moves or the song you pick to boogie down to. Let the music take control and just go with it. Feel like doing the electric slide? Do it. Want to practice your running man? There's no time like the present!

Take Your Vitamins

Your body is a temple, and it needs the proper nourishment to stay strong and healthy. Fire signs are constantly pushing their physical limits by taking on new athletic challenges. To keep your body from getting run-down, it's important to stick to a vitamin regimen every day. Talk to your doctor about which vitamins are best for you. There are even companies that offer personalized vitamin packs based on your individual needs. Even just a simple multivitamin made for your age group or gender can give your body the boost it needs.

Volunteer Your Time

L eo is a generous soul. Put this wonderful trait to good use by volunteering your time.

Seek out a charity aligned with causes you are most passionate about. While national charities do a lot of good work, in your own town you'll find local charities looking for helpful hands. Animal shelters, hospital and hospice services, and organizations serving children or the environment are great places to start.

Additionally, keep an eye out for neighbors who could use a helping hand. Offer to take a senior citizen's trash cans back up the driveway after garbage day. Shovel snow from the walk of a home where you know young children live. No act is too small—it will make a difference to both your day and the day of the recipient.

Try an Extreme Sport

Leo is an adventurous, daring spirit. Feed your thirst for excitement by trying an extreme sport. Love the water? Try scuba diving, wakeboarding, waterskiing, or kitesurfing. Want to see things through a bird's-eye view? Try rock or wall climbing, skydiving, bungee jumping, or parasailing. If you want to stay closer to the ground, try BMX bicycling, trail running, in-line skating, skateboarding, or paintballing.

No matter what you pick, you'll get the adrenaline flowing and get some exercise in!

Stargaze

The universe is expansive. Just look up at the sky on a pitch-black night. There are tiny suns and balls of flaming gas millions of miles away. Some estimates suggest there are approximately one hundred billion stars in just the Milky Way alone. Imagine how many more there are in the billions of other galaxies in the universe.

Your presence in this universe is important. Never lose the passion and heat you have burning inside you as a fire sign. It can be easy to feel small sometimes. When you are feeling lost, look up at the stars. They can help you find your way. And if you are lucky, you may even discover the constellations of one of the fire signs—Aries, Leo, or Sagittarius—to guide you.

Run for Local Government

―――――――――――

A t his best Leo is confident and assertive; he thrives in the spotlight and leads with generosity. He is a powerful speaker. Why not put these qualities to good use by running for a position in local government?

While you may not consider yourself a political mind, think about your strengths and areas of interest. Are you passionate about animals? Do you love working on behalf of children? Are you a passionate reader? Are you dedicated to fighting for the environment? There are positions in animal control, libraries, schools, and preservation that could be a good fit for your Leo passion and confidence.

While it may not be a role you envisioned for yourself, you never know where your talents could take you—and how they can positively contribute to the world around you.

Go to a Music Festival

Surround yourself with creativity at a music festival.

Leo will fit in well in this eclectic scene—it's an opportunity to spend time in the sunshine, socialize, and appreciate music. While Leo may be most comfortable on stage, dancing with friends in your favorite concert wear is a close second. Music festivals are a wonderful place to express yourself freely, and flamboyancy is welcome in this "anything goes" environment.

Organize a group of friends, and make it a point to attend a festival this concert season. Between enjoying good music sets, you'll be able to connect with your friends and possibly make new ones. This vibrant scene is a wonderful place to enjoy an act of self-care.

Brew a Pot of Sun Tea

Harness the energy of the sun and enjoy it at any time—indoors or out, in the hot or cold weather—by brewing and enjoy a fresh pot of sun tea.

This flavorful brew is an excellent way to feed Leo's innate desire for the sun. To make sun tea, simply place eight tea bags in a clean and clear gallon glass container. Fill the container with water and screw on the top. Place the container outdoors in a spot where it will get good sunlight. Keep in the sun for 3 to 5 hours, moving the container if necessary to keep it in the sunlight.

Enjoy this sun-fueled beverage any time you could use a dose of sunshine!

About the Author

Constance Stellas is an astrologer of Greek heritage with more than twenty-five years of experience. She primarily practices in New York City and counsels a variety of clients, including business CEOs, artists, and scholars. She has been interviewed by *The New York Times*, *Marie Claire*, and *Working Woman*, and has appeared on several New York TV morning shows, featuring regularly on Sirius XM and other national radio programs as well. Constance is the astrologer for *HuffPost* and a regular contributor to Thrive Global. She is also the author of several titles, including *The Astrology Gift Guide*, *Advanced Astrology for Life*, *The Everything® Sex Signs Book*, and the graphic novel series Tree of Keys, as well as coauthor of *The Hidden Power of Everyday Things*. Learn more about Constance at her website, ConstanceStellas.com, or on *Twitter* (@Stellastarguide).